Marissa Higgins' *Shopgirls* celebrates the grotesque with unexpected delight. Higgins' precise syllables and subtle alliteration will make you hungry. Flesh, bone, and expectation, *Shopgirls* is unafraid of breaking and lingering in the resulting pain. You are about to witness the work of a highly skilled surgeon.

—Danielle Evennou author of *Difficult Trick*

How does one negotiate self-preservation in the throes of desire? How do you defamiliarize the familiar that you may understand the self better? Early in Marissa Higgins' chapbook, *Shopgirls*, the speaker reveals, "I've learned how to preserve/ what remains," and these poems acutely distill the exchange of power dynamics as enrapture defines its own terms. "Don't you know/ what it is to work for love?" we are asked—and haven't "My attempts to please" also been "slow" at times, haven't my fingers reached for something just out of reach, haven't I "[wiggled]/ like a panicked thing, smaller/than a deer or God" in my wantings? With concision—and precision—Higgins refuses to shy away from the body in desire, leaving the reader wanting also to be "even closer to what is/ and was pleasure."

—Flower Conroy author of *The Awful Suicidal Swans*

In *Shopgirls*, Marissa Higgins creates a world that explores human insecurity by juxtaposing fashion and science. The "anatomy" of her poems "bulging beneath denim" "wound[s] in ways [Higgins] does not know how to heal." It is tight poetry that "takes [you] from behind" and forces "bruise[s] to blossom." It is an emotionally charged volume that pushes our perceptions about capitalism and our bodies to new levels—a genuine vivisection.

—Jessica Hylton author of *The Great Scissor Hunt*

Shopgirls

Shopgirls

Marissa Higgins

HEADMISTRESS PRESS

Copyright © 2018 by Marissa Higgins
All rights reserved.

ISBN-13: 978-0998761091
ISBN-10: 0998761095

This book may not be reproduced, in whole or in part, including illustrations, in any form (beyond that permitted by Sections 107 and 108 of the U.S. Copyright Law and except by reviewers for the public press), without written permission from the publishers.

Cover art by Jeanne Mammen, *Revue Girls* (1928-1929). Public Domain.
Cover & book design by Mary Meriam.

PUBLISHER
Headmistress Press
60 Shipview Lane
Sequim, WA 98382
Telephone: 917-428-8312
Email: headmistresspress@gmail.com
Website: headmistresspress.blogspot.com

Contents

On Weigh-Ins and Wanting	1
The Wellness Visit	3
The Downsizing	4
Before The Trains Stop Running	5
Ten Minutes Till Close	6
How To Care For A Collarbone	7
On The Anticipation Of Touch	8
Before Temperance	9
The Feast	10
The Sell	11
When Time is Soft and Steady	12
The Closet	13
The Dressing Room	14
While The Security Guard Sleeps	15
Bacterial Design	16
On Disconnections	17
On Doubt	18
Until Further Notice	19
On Begrudging Rebirth	20
The Distance	21
Second Delivery Attempt	22
A Quiet Maturation	23
On Creation	24
Acknowledgments	25
About the Author	27

On Weigh-Ins and Wanting

Your elbows are looking mighty
fine today, the salesgirl said,
measuring tape in hand,

numbers more legitimate
than the eye. I thanked her

and cracked one
off, careful to split
below my brachialis.

I've learned how to preserve
what remains, not young enough

now to fracture.
My attempts to please
are slow.

I miss eye-work days,
when the salesgirl sliced my lids,

plucked my lashes
from their stems
to assess in her petri dish.

I got them from my mother,
I whispered once

thinking of where
this body derives.
Oh, she said, they weigh two ounces

each. Not having an elbow
is funny, you know, I can't

straighten
or bend
or break

but my fingers,
they reach,

they reach.

The Wellness Visit

The stockroom boasts shoes in boxes
coats on hangers, fingers in gloves
hips left in jeans skinny   not
quite enough

to pull, push, wiggle
like a panicked thing, smaller
than a deer or God

my salesgirl steams each
pore, my face an open
palette, she promises moisture
makes for a cleaner cut.

The Downsizing

In my morning fitting,
my salesgirl slick
slices scissors
me, side to side

my ribs an aching
greeting, one left
one right, excised,
bagged, today she is

gentle with her thrusts
pleasant with her stitches

Before The Trains Stop Running

my salesgirl hovers above
aisles, shimmies
curls pops
orchestrates

me, encrusted,
embalmed, enraptured

Ten Minutes Till Close

The salesgirl takes me
from behind

two other waiting women
wanting to be plucked, pulled, popped

we pass a man with an engorged
tongue   useless in his mouth

she commands me in routine:
sit, squat, kneel, bend, roll

hip to jaw
knee to navel

even the mannequins watch

How To Care For A Collarbone

the shop finally shuts
up, and i breathe her
furtive, barely coy
*

my salesgirl circles
my smallness, somehow
it sustains, survives
*

when bruised, remember:
use fingertips, avoid
palms—expansive, brute

On The Anticipation Of Touch

my salesgirl suspends me
from a hanger meant
for skirts or narrow
people

ankles to shoulder
my stomach ripples once
mostly skin and a little bit
of fat, i want her

to say that she missed
those cells remaining
from girlhood, pre-light
beers, post-ice cream,

she inspects me for agitation,
waits for me to ripen,
soften like a peach retired
at the bottom of my purse

i want her to devour my whole
damn body, mostly
want her to harvest
and scream.

Before Temperance

My salesgirl appraises me
in her usual ways:

temperature, rate of hair growth,
girth of tendon, how long it takes a bruise

to blossom. When she is done, she slices
two freckles from my left lobe, the secret

skin we love to fondle. Days later she sucks
puss from the scab and I churn delight

full of finite self and understanding,
all caught in fluorescent embrace.

The Feast

Today, the security guard
uses his gun, no bullets,

just length, to still me
in the door, eyes inside out,

anatomy bulging
beneath denim.

I grin like a creature lesser
than giants, smarter than mice

and he motions for me to open
my mouth. My tongue engorged

from shopgirl nibbles, from
gnaws alone in my big white room,

titillates his hope and he lets me pass
through him, surveilling without protecting.

The Sell

The counter is cluttered: knee caps,
sprained toes, thirteen freckles smiling
while my salesgirl pathologizes
this blistered wrist it is mine
so green ever I think at least
my carpal bones are dainty
and weary they have travelled
for my salesgirl she sets
their value she weighs
their worth my carpus aches
lonely, suddenly—
it is the first place any woman loved.

When Time Is Soft And Steady

My vertebra relaxes
into an ache, smolders
against a register, locked
with a key composed
of molded teeth. I wait
willingly, occupied
with hope and calm
obsession. My salesgirl
takes care not to wound
in ways she doesn't know
how to heal. Beneath me
the floor whimpers life;
my tailbone erupts
a mighty canyon.

The Closet

in the corner, behind a broom
my salesgirl sits small

unlike how I know her,
all papercuts and peroxide.

I strip, offer her my
knee, elbow, left hip

right eyebrow, lashes
on the lower lids,

the ones she loved
to name. She hands me

an empty glass, folds
knees into neck,

reveals the bottom of her
feet: a small gift.

She spits up receipts,
lists, memos, itineraries,

evidence of shadow.

The Dressing Room

My salesgirl dictates
my reflection, no intercom
just her words from
above. In our early days,

her evaluations followed
script: length of hip, agility
of tongue, malleability
of bone. When she loves

me, evaluations bend
my body, always hips
neck, knees, jaw. Today
my mirror is her shadow,

her distance too separate
from anger for me to correct.
We hover in silence,
changelings us both.

While The Security Guard Sleeps

My salesgirl eats
her tongue, chews

in rhythm with the ceiling
clocks. She is beautiful

in the display window, higher than I
remember, closer to God

than not. I arch my heels, wave
like she has come back from war

or another lover. She opens herself
and reveals a mighty pulp. Her tongue

sweats blood. I put mine between
my teeth, nibble twice

before she swallows herself
and closes shop.

Bacterial Design

I wait beside the dumpsters
watch my salesgirl separate
cells, previously self-organized
into colonies, seeking
survival. Tonight, my salesgirl
is fickle. She flicks her
fingers and self-protection
dies. I tongue my insides,
mostly my left cheek,
still sore from yesterday's
probes. My salesgirl evaporates
with the humidity; from inside
the dumpster, I hear my body
scream.

On Disconnections

After the beep, my salesgirl
sings numbers, odd
then even, only
negatives. I slither
through the mouth
piece to watch her
sort hangers, sweep
hair and knuckles,
water plants that watch
from the ceiling. I envy
their moxy; unashamed,
they hang and dry, reminders
of vulnerability, of our promises
to tend.

On Doubt

Three large plants dressed
in burlap watch me
wait whimper wilt
while my salesgirl takes
stock: seven sets of eye
lashes, coordinated pair
of breasts, firmer than
mangos from April
or July, one canine painted
pink with polish, relics
from other girls she
met across the counter.

One ankle sits in the sun.
Its smallness usurps,
consumes, this home.

Until Further Notice

I model my salesgirl
out of dust, stitch her
in time with my emissions:
sodium, phosphate,
calcium, iron, chloride,
cervical mucus, endometrial
tissues. My soft secretions
remind me: there are no returns
today.

On Begrudging Rebirth

Today, I try the new shop
on the corner of west and fourth,
two blocks north of where my salesgirl
opened and closed

me. Inside, everything is special:
half-price, half-value, half-human—
I am ready to fall in love again
to replace this meager carcass.

My new salesgirl advertises
all that I seek: slight hands, big
breasts, sad eyes that hunger
for healing,

the only love I know
how to generate. She wants me
for submission, the cellulite
on my right thigh, the lumped

joints of my fingers. Her kindness,
too tender; artifice stings
like a proud blister. My rejection:
uneasy, sloppy, soft.

*Don't you know what it is to work
for love?* She scrapes my hair
for testing, nails to scalp.
I'm unwilling, now, to give

the cells that still burst
and churn and feel.

The Distance

Beneath my mattress,
I curl into myself;
small, brittle warmth.

Second Delivery Attempt

I awake cradled
in her left ear the fifth
pore swaddles me with heat
sweat and dirt, I embrace
myself, sing numbers even,
then odd, titillate

her ear remembers
not, but the follicles remind,
they demand relief
in the clutch of nails

I infiltrate

A Quiet Maturation

My salesgirl folds me
into a box for safe
keeping she ties a bow

it is her hair, the thread,
the scent, it is honeysuckle, it gives
me comfort like milk, like distance

as I make love to moths
and wax and dust.

On Creation

Below the crack in the right
corner of the second dressing

room on the first floor, just
above where the tile pulls

up against your bare, bare
feet my salesgirl left a lever

for me to pull twice—the second time
required, in the event of hesitance,

or whims—and release our bodies,
her Frankensteins, soft caricatures

the clerks and customers can place
on either side of the counter

as I pass through and return myself
to where she is, where I have never

been, I see her goodness
in my double, the curve of my

nostrils, the long, loving hair
curled off-center of the mole

on my left thigh: the place
she loved most to smell.

Her ancestors must've been
carpenters or God, or something

even closer to what is
and was pleasure.

Acknowledgments

Thanks to the editors of the following publications, in which these poems first appeared:

Calamus: "Ten Minutes Till Close"

Noble/Gas Quarterly: "How to Care for a Collarbone"

Softblow: "On Weigh-Ins and Wanting," "On The Anticipation of Touch," "The Feast," "The Dressing Room"

About the Author

Marissa Higgins is a writer and editor living in Washington, DC. She is an associate editor at *Green Matters,* where she covers green news and sustainability. In her freelance work, she centers on poverty, class, queer issues, and women's health.

Her personal essays have appeared in the *Washington Post, Guernica, Salon,* Gertrude Press, and *Catapult.* Her reported work has appeared in the *Atlantic, Pacific Standard, NPR, Complex, Slate, Teen Vogue,* and beyond. Formerly, she wrote for *Bustle* in the Lifestyle section, and covered trending news for the *Daily Dot* and *Refinery29*.

Her poetry has appeared in *Apogee, Rogue Agent, Bone Bouquet, Softblow,* and *Calamus Journal.* SHOPGIRLS is her first book.

Headmistress Press Books

Lovely - Lesléa Newman
Teeth & Teeth - Robin Reagler
How Distant the City - Freesia McKee
Shopgirls - Marissa Higgins
Riddle - Diane Fortney
When She Woke She Was an Open Field - Hilary Brown
God With Us - Amy Lauren
A Crown of Violets - Renée Vivien tr. Samantha Pious
Fireworks in the Graveyard - Joy Ladin
Social Dance - Carolyn Boll
The Force of Gratitude - Janice Gould
Spine - Sarah Caulfield
Diatribe from the Library - Farrell Greenwald Brenner
Blind Girl Grunt - Constance Merritt
Acid and Tender - Jen Rouse
Beautiful Machinery - Wendy DeGroat
Odd Mercy - Gail Thomas
The Great Scissor Hunt - Jessica K. Hylton
A Bracelet of Honeybees - Lynn Strongin
Whirlwind @ Lesbos - Risa Denenberg
The Body's Alphabet - Ann Tweedy
First name Barbie last name Doll - Maureen Bocka
Heaven to Me - Abe Louise Young
Sticky - Carter Steinmann
Tiger Laughs When You Push - Ruth Lehrer
Night Ringing - Laura Foley
Paper Cranes - Dinah Dietrich
On Loving a Saudi Girl - Carina Yun
The Burn Poems - Lynn Strongin
I Carry My Mother - Lesléa Newman
Distant Music - Joan Annsfire
The Awful Suicidal Swans - Flower Conroy
Joy Street - Laura Foley
Chiaroscuro Kisses - G.L. Morrison
The Lillian Trilogy - Mary Meriam
Lady of the Moon - Amy Lowell, Lillian Faderman, Mary Meriam
Irresistible Sonnets - ed. Mary Meriam
Lavender Review - ed. Mary Meriam

www.ingramcontent.com/pod-product-compliance
Lightning Source LLC
Chambersburg PA
CBHW070045070426
42449CB00012BA/3165